Everything You Need To Know About

TEEN

SUICIDE

Everything You Need To Know About

TEEN
SUICIDE

Jay Schleifer

Series Editor: Evan Stark, Ph.D.

THE ROSEN PUBLISHING GROUP, INC.
NEW YORK

Published in 1988, 1991, 1993 by The Rosen Publishing Group, Inc.
29 East 21st Street, New York, New York 10010

Revised Edition 1993
Copyright © 1988, 1991, 1993 by The Rosen Publishing Group, Inc.

Manufactured in the United States of America.

Library of Congress Cataloging-in-Publication Data

Schleifer, Jay
    Everything you need to know about teen suicide / Jay Schleifer.
    (The need to know library)
    Includes bibliographical references and index.
    Summary: Examines reasons why young people kill themselves, how
to recognise when friends are in such trouble, and how to help potential
suicide victims.
    ISBN 0-8239-1612-X
    1. Teenagers—United States—Suicidal behavior—Juvenile literature.
2. Suicide—United States—Prevention—Juvenile literature. [1. Suicide]
I. Title. II. Series.
HV6546.S36   1988
362.2—dc19   **3 5944 00036 3505**   88-6636
                                                          CIP
                                                             AC

Contents

Introduction 6

1. "How Could I Know?" 9

2. Teen Suicide: Facts and Myths 12

3. Why It Happens 23

4. Warning Signs 37

5. Getting Help 43

6. "I Feel Like I Want to Kill Myself" 49

7. Healing and Hope 53

Glossary-Explaining New Words 59

Where to Go for Help 60

For Further Reading 61

Index 63

Introduction

There are many reasons to read this book. Maybe you know someone who has taken his or her own life. Or maybe you've thought about it yourself.

Maybe you know someone who has *tried* to commit suicide. Researchers say that each day, over 700 people between the ages of 15 and 24 try to kill themselves.

If you do know someone who has tried to commit suicide, you should know that there is a risk that he or she might try again. But there are other signs to look for in people who are considering suicide. These people might:

○ say they want to die, or that they're thinking about killing themselves.

○ suddenly start giving away things that are important to them (such as their favorite books or CDs).
○ abuse alcohol or drugs.
○ become very moody—"up" one minute and "down" the next.
○ become very withdrawn, pulling away from their friends and family.
○ take lots of unnecessary risks (such as driving recklessly, or drinking and driving).

Teen suicide is a very sad, and very serious, problem. But one of the saddest things about it is that most people who try to kill themselves *do not truly want to die.* They may feel that they can't go on living. What they need is to know that someone cares.

If you think someone you know is considering suicide, *ask him or her!* Don't be afraid. If this person says he or she *is* thinking about it, there are people you can call for help!

○ A suicide hotline
○ A hospital
○ A school counselor, teacher, or youth worker
○ The police
○ A minister, priest, or rabbi

You won't be putting ideas into your friend's head by bringing it up. If you have the courage to talk about suicide, you might help to save a life.

Chapter 1

"How Could I Know?"

Cindy Norris looked out the window of the school bus. There was Joe, walking in the rain. He was coming home from being out all night.

Joe lived next door. They had grown up together. Joe often gave Cindy rides on the back of his Honda motorcycle.

But Joe had changed. Now he was always alone. He didn't come by her house anymore. He didn't joke with her in school. And he was always taking these night walks. It seemed as if he never went to bed.

Now Joe saw Cindy in the bus and waved. That made her feel better. But he was so thin. He was smoking cigarettes more than he ever did. And he never played ball after school anymore.

But the funniest thing was giving away his Honda. One day he just handed the keys to his friend Mike. He just said, "Take care of it. I don't deserve to have it anymore. I don't deserve anything."

After school the bus dropped Cindy off at the end of her block. She could see the headlights even from there. Two police cars were parked in front of Joe's house. Cindy asked a neighbor, Mrs. Nelson, what was going on.

"Didn't you hear, Cindy?" asked Mrs. Nelson. "Joe Barlow killed himself. He jumped off the railroad bridge down at Factory Street. The police found his body on the tracks. His parents found a note in his room at home. He said he had broken up with a girl and fumbled a ball in a big game. Just think! Seventeen years old and he kills himself over that. Crazy, just crazy."

This book is about young people like Joe who kill themselves. It's about their friends like Cindy. Cindy knew something was wrong. But she didn't know what to do.

All young people feel lonely, sad, and anxious at times. It is a normal part of growing up. But for some, these feelings can become very powerful. A teen may feel helpless. He or she may start to see suicide as the only way out. But choosing death is never a solution to a problem. It is only an escape.

At one time, suicide was considered a disgrace. In parts of Europe, people who killed themselves were often buried at a crossroads. This was intended to draw attention and shame to the suicide. For many years, suicide was considered a crime in some parts of the United States.

Many movies, plays, and books tell stories about teens who killed themselves. Remember the two young lovers in Shakespeare's *Romeo and Juliet*? They each took their own life when they thought the other was dead.

But suicide is not romantic or glamorous. It helps no one. Young people can be very unhappy at times. But they may not truly want to die. They may need to know that someone cares. They may need to be shown that they have other choices. They need to be encouraged to choose life.

This book will tell you more about why some young people may *think* they want to die. It will also tell you about ways you can help.

Chapter 2

Teen Suicide: Facts and Myths

In recent years, many people have become more concerned about teen suicide. About 6,000 young Americans kill themselves each year. That number is more than *three times* higher than the number of teen suicides in America 30 years ago. Among people between the ages of 15 and 19, suicide is the third leading cause of death. One survey found that 1 out of every 12 American high-school students *tried* to commit suicide in 1990.

Suicide is always tragic. But it is especially sad when a *young* person decides that life is not worth living. That person's friends and family will feel pain and grief for the rest of their lives.

In Texas, students get together to discuss common problems. During one six-month period in this town six teens attempted suicide.

After every teen suicide, grief-stricken friends try to understand how someone they knew and loved could have such strong feelings. How could it happen without anyone else knowing or being able to help? School counselors and teachers grieve too. They know that such a death could almost certainly have been prevented. Counseling, or "crisis intervention," can save lives. But people must be aware in order to help.

What Makes Teens Feel So Bad?

It is not possible to list all the reasons why teens decide to take their own lives. But here are some of the more common causes:

- Feeling rejected, abandoned, or alone
- Low self-esteem, or feeling like a failure
- Feeling ashamed, unworthy of forgiveness
- Pressures at school, home, or with friends
- Problems with alcohol or drugs
- Feelings of hopelessness or depression (sadness that does not go away and has no clear cause)
- Feeling afraid of something or someone

Often teens who kill themselves have had upsetting experiences of some kind. Young suicide victims may leave notes behind when they die. They list reasons like these:

○ Breaking up with a boyfriend or girlfriend
○ Doing poorly in school, or not being accepted for a job or by a college
○ Not doing well in sports or other activities
○ Moving and leaving friends behind, or having a good friend move away
○ Divorce or other problems in the family (such as alcohol, drugs or sexual abuse)
○ Being unable to repay a large debt
○ A serious physical injury or illness
○ Being responsible for an injury to another person
○ Having committed a serious crime
○ The death of a parent, close friend, or other family member

It's not easy being a teen. Some of the problems teen suicide victims list may seem much more serious than others. But all of these problems are very real to the people who experience them.

These problems can also trigger some of the uncomfortable feelings we listed first. For example, a parents' divorce may make a teen feel rejected and abandoned. He or she may not be able to cope with new pressures at home. The teen years are full of powerful and confusing emotions that can last a long time.

Young people who say they want to die often think these painful feelings will never go away. They are wrong. Bad feelings can go away. It may not be easy to work through these feelings. And it will probably take time. But it *is* possible to get help and turn your life around. For teens who are deeply troubled, there is no time to waste. For them, it may be a matter of life or death.

Accident—or Suicide?

Maybe more teenagers kill themselves than we know. That is because some deaths are not called suicide.

The police say that a 17-year-old in Texas died when he was fooling around with his father's gun. The gun went off and killed him. But some people thought it looked very funny. The lights in the boy's room were turned off. The gun was pointed right at his head. And there was a bottle of liquor beside him that was half empty. Was it an accident? Some people thought it was suicide.

People also wonder about some car accidents. A young person is alone in the car and crashes into something. The teen is killed. But nothing was wrong with the car. Was it an accident? Maybe.

In one of America's largest cities, a nine-year-old boy tried to jump out of his fourth-floor classroom window. Some experts have begun to ask whether young children who fall from tall buildings wanted to kill themselves. We are learning that problems can cause great pain for some people even before the teen years.

A few minutes after this picture was taken, this young man
jumped to his death.

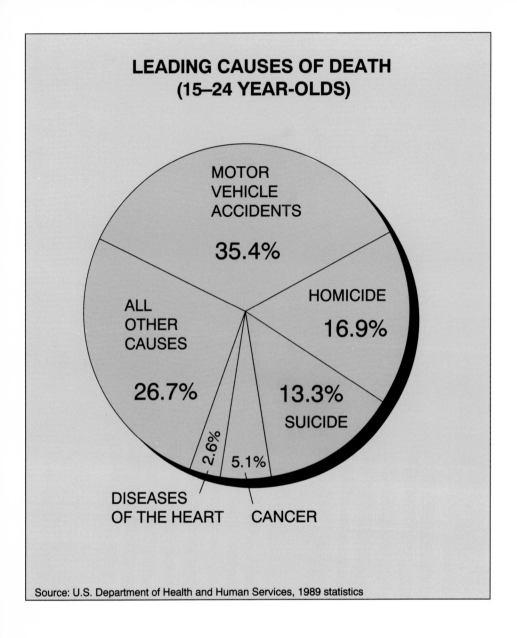

**LEADING CAUSES OF DEATH
(15–24 YEAR-OLDS)**

MOTOR
VEHICLE
ACCIDENTS

35.4%

HOMICIDE

16.9%

ALL
OTHER
CAUSES

26.7%

13.3%

SUICIDE

2.6%

5.1%

DISEASES
OF THE HEART   CANCER

Source: U.S. Department of Health and Human Services, 1989 statistics

Many families are ashamed if a child takes his or her own life. They feel that it says something bad about them. So they try to make it look like an accident.

But teen suicide is on the rise. People need to know and face the truth about suicide. Maybe then it will be easier to stop it.

Don't You Believe It

When you hear the word *myth* you think of a story about imaginary people or events. We also use the term myth to refer to a mistaken belief or idea. This kind of myth can be harmful because it can prevent people from taking actions they should take. The following are a few of the common myths about teen suicide.

Young people who talk about killing themselves never really do.

This is a dangerous idea. Eight out of ten suicide victims tell someone they are planning to take their own lives. If someone you know says he or she is considering suicide, you should take it seriously. This person needs immediate help. You should encourage him or her to talk to an adult they can trust. Or you could go to someone like a teacher, school counselor, minister or rabbi for advice. They will be able to tell you how to help your friend.

Suicides usually happen without warning.

This myth is related to the first one. Most of the time, young people who are thinking about suicide *do* let someone know. If they don't say so directly, they might give out certain hints. For example, a teenager who is thinking about suicide might start giving away important personal belongings. He or she might start taking lots of unnecessary risks. In Chapter 4 we talk more about some of the "warning signs" of suicide.

If someone really wants to commit suicide, no one can talk them out of it.

This is a very harmful myth, too. Remember, people who are thinking about suicide often do *not* truly want to die. What they need is for someone to show that they care. They need to know they are not alone, even though it may feel like they are. Don't give up on teens who are considering suicide. They *can* and *should* be talked out of it if at all possible.

A person who seems to get better after trying to commit suicide will never try to kill himself or herself again.

Unfortunately, this is not the case. People who have tried suicide before are at risk of trying again. This does not mean that everyone who failed the first time will try again. But it does mean that anyone who has attempted suicide will need a lot of concern and support afterwards.

Talking about suicide with an unhappy person can create dangerous ideas. Talking about it might cause him or her to try it.

If you think someone is considering suicide, you should always talk to him or her about it. You

Police try to find out why four teens committed suicide.

won't be putting ideas into their head. Remember, these young people *need* to talk about their unhappiness. People who are thinking about suicide believe that no one knows or cares about how they feel. They need to be told that they are important. Your concern may give them strength to overcome their problems or find professional help.

Suicide is hereditary. If someone in your family commits suicide, you are likely to do the same thing.

This myth can make young people frightened and confused. If someone in your family commits suicide, this can certainly lead to feelings of depression and helplessness. But this does not mean you will want to take your own life, too. While strong feelings may run in families, suicide does not.

A powerful feeling of "aloneness" is sometimes the first sign of trouble.

Chapter 3

Why It Happens

It was more than a month since Emily's Aunt Jane had died. She had been killed in a car accident. Emily's Aunt Jane had been more like a best friend than a relative. Emily was fifteen. Aunt Jane was only twenty-three.

Aunt Jane was the person Emily talked to about all her problems. And Aunt Jane always helped her figure things out and start to feel better. They liked the same music. They borrowed each other's clothes. They went to movies and concerts together. They went on vacations together every summer.

Now Aunt Jane was gone. Emily could not have felt more alone. Every song she liked reminded her of Aunt Jane. And she would never see Aunt Jane again. Without her, Emily did not want to live.

Bob looked at the clock by his bed. The time was 2:14 A.M. and he still couldn't get to sleep. Bob knew why, all right. All year he had been messing up in school. He failed tests. He lost his homework. He never understood the teacher. It seemed that he could never win.

But this time his father was really mad. If he got one more letter from the school, said Dad, Bob would be in big trouble. He couldn't use the car. His allowance would stop. He would be grounded at home. And now Bob knew that the principal had written to Dad again!

Bob knew what he had to do. He had thought about it many times. He knew where the gun was kept. He knew how to load and lock it, and how to fire it. By the time the mail came tomorrow, his bad grades wouldn't matter anymore.

Kelly and Tom! Somehow those names belonged together. At least, that's what Kelly thought. How she loved Tom! She dreamed how they would be married right after high school. She made plans for where they would live. She chose names for the two kids they would have.

But Tom had other ideas. One day he told Kelly that he was getting bored. And he had decided that the cure for his boredom was Janet, Kelly's best friend. "But I can't live without you!" Kelly had sobbed. "Sorry," said Tom. "I guess you'll have to learn to."

A rose and some photographs were all two young women left behind when they committed suicide. They left the motor running in a closed garage.

The pain felt by a suicide's family
never goes away.

No, I won't! thought Kelly. Tom would have to learn that. And so would Janet. And the way to teach them was the bottle of pills in the bathroom cabinet.

The Power of Feelings

Three teens had strong feelings. One was lonely. One had bad grades. One had broken up with a boyfriend. Maybe all of them had reasons to cry. But were they reasons to die? Most people wouldn't think so. But these three teens did. Why?

What is the same about all their stories?

For one thing, all three had strong feelings. Emily felt sad and lonely. Bob felt fear. Kelly felt anger and loss of hope. Their feelings were all different. But they were all strong enough to change the thoughts of the young people. Their feelings shut off the way they usually thought, the way static drowns out a song on the radio.

Can feelings be that strong? Can they change the way a person thinks? The answer is yes. Even animals can show how this can happen.

At night an animal may get caught in the headlights of a car. Animals aren't as intelligent as people. But they are smart enough to run when a car comes at them fast. And that is what they do in the daylight. At night, though, they don't understand the bright light. It fills them with fear. They are frozen by fear. They just stand in the road. The idea of running away is blocked off. Unless the driver of the car stops, the animal will die.

People, too, can become frozen by their feelings. They can be blocked off from their usual ways of thinking. This is called a mental block.

If Emily could think normally, she would know that her Aunt Jane wanted her to have a long and full life. Bob would decide that he could stand being grounded for a while. Kelly would realize that she could easily find a new love.

But they were not thinking normally. Their minds were blocked. They each saw their problem as hopeless. They all saw only one way out.

When normal thinking is blocked by feelings, people have an emotional reaction. And that kind of reaction is most likely to happen when the person is having a crisis.

Time of Crisis

A *crisis* is a time when things get as bad as they can be. Problems build up until they reach a breaking point. When this happens, things will either start to turn around and get better, or end with a tragedy.

Think about when you are sick. If your fever rises higher and higher, you feel worse and worse as time passes. After a while, you may reach a

A teen's emotions may often feel like a roller coaster ride.

crisis level in your illness. At this point, if your fever continues it could result in convulsions (violent muscle spasms beyond your control). But if your fever breaks, you begin to recover and start to feel better.

An unhappy teen may have problems that build up until he/she reaches a personal crisis. It may begin with a problem at home. An alcoholic parent, for example, may be out of work and difficult to live with. The teen's family problems may result in other problems at school. With added stress the teen may turn to drugs as an escape. As the problems get even more serious the teen may be headed for a crisis.

Many young people are tested. Everyone has problems. Most teens are strong enough to handle a crisis situation. Teens with good self-esteem believe in their own ability to solve problems. They also know they can find help if they need it. They take control of their own lives.

Unfortunately, not all young people have a healthy self-image. They may lack courage and confidence at the time of a crisis. They may feel helpless. They may also not be able to control the other feelings that go along with a crisis.

As a young person feels worse about what is happening in the family, he/she may also feel *angry*. He/she may feel *fear* about the future. He/she may feel *ashamed* and not want anyone to know.

The young adult also may feel *guilty*. He/she may think, "Maybe it's my fault. Maybe it's because of something I did. Maybe it's something I didn't do."

Feeling helpless in a crisis can make a young person think about suicide. Deciding on suicide can make someone feel calm. They no longer feel helpless, because they have decided to act. Others may think that the young person is getting better. Friends or family may decide that the person no longer needs help. Then the person is really in danger. Soon, if no one steps in to help, the suicidal teenager may try to end his/her life.

The truth is, things *could* get better for this young person. But teenagers who think they want

Sometimes we all feel very "up"—like the roller coaster at the top of its climb.

to die cannot see this on their own. When they reach a crisis, they need someone to reach out and show them a better way.

Chemicals Make a Difference

Times of crisis happen in all our lives. They may not be as bad as the breakup of a family. They may be that bad or even worse. But most people do not try to deal with them by killing themselves. Most people know that somehow they will solve the problems and go on living. They know that the roller coaster will stay on the track. They are sure that at the bottom of the hill the ride will level out and end where it began.

Why can't the suicidal teenager understand this too?

It is because the emotion blocks such thoughts. And the more emotional a person is, the stronger the reaction will be.

No one knows why some people are more emotional than others. But it is easy to see that it is true. Look at the people at a rock concert or a big football game. Some people just sit there and watch. Others jump up and down and scream and shout.

We think that this difference may be caused by having different amounts of certain chemicals in the brain. Maybe the amount of those chemicals a person has is inherited from his or her parents. That does not mean that if you or your parents are very emotional, you are also suicidal. It does mean that you need to understand yourself and your feelings. You need to know that those powerful feelings might keep you from making good decisions.

Cluster Suicides

In recent years, there have been a number of *cluster suicides*. In cluster suicides (also called "copycat suicides"), one or more troubled teens imitate another young person who has committed suicide. They "copy" that person by killing themselves in the same or similar way.

Everyone was very sad when young Steven Smith, a high school sports star, took his own life. He breathed carbon monoxide from the exhaust of the family car. But the sadness didn't end there. Soon afterward another student at the same school took her life in the same way.

Cluster suicides have happened in many towns across the country. The TV news reports a death in one state. Suddenly there are deaths like it thousands of miles away.

Copycat suicide doesn't even have to imitate an actual death. Even a story on TV about teenage suicide can be followed by the real thing.

Looking for Attention

Teens often see suicide as a way to get attention. They see it as a way to be famous. But they don't understand that they won't be around to enjoy the attention or the fame. You don't come back from being dead. But teens thinking about suicide don't really understand that. You may never have felt depressed enough to think about suicide. The idea of trying to get attention that way may not make sense to you. But teens who are depressed do not think clearly. They are confused.

We started this chapter looking for the reasons that teens kill themselves. The newspapers often say the reason was trouble at home or at school. But millions of teenagers have such problems without trying suicide. The real reason must be something else. It must be the combination of a crisis in life and a young person who cannot think clearly about it.

Another part of the trouble is with other people. The people who care for the young person don't know the signs that a suicide may be coming. They don't know what to do if they see those signs.

Luckily, you can learn how to spot the signs of suicide. You know how to get help when you see them. The next two chapters will tell you how.

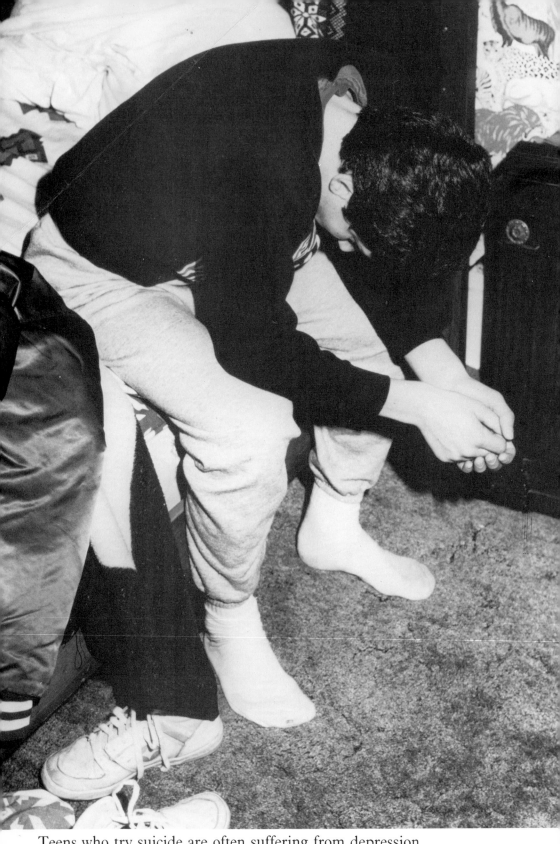
Teens who try suicide are often suffering from depression.

Chapter 4

Warning Signs

T his book began with the story of Cindy Norris and Joe Barlow. When Cindy learned of Joe's death, she asked herself, "How could I know?"

Joe sent out at least six signs that something was terribly wrong. At least one of those signs said that he was thinking of taking his own life.

Almost all people thinking about suicide send out signs of the way they are feeling. Usually they do not want to die. They want help. They try to let the world know they need help.

These signs are very helpful in trying to end teenage suicide. The more young people learn about the signs, the more chance they will have of preventing suicide when a friend is in trouble.

Cries for Help

Sometimes, unhappy teens send very clear signals that they think they want to die. Here are some to watch for.

Trying to commit suicide.

The most obvious warning that a teen is suicidal is when the teen actually tries to take his or her life. Even if the attempt at suicide fails, it is important. Just because someone has tried once and failed, that does not mean he or she won't try again. Anyone at this crisis point is at great risk. Getting help immediately is the only hope for making a lasting recovery.

Making threats: talking about suicide.

If someone you know says they are considering suicide, you should take them seriously. Most people who try to kill themselves tell someone, at some point, that they are thinking about it. Be a friend. Listen first, then get help.

Giving out clues.

Often, a young person who is thinking about suicide will talk a lot about death. They may not talk about their *own* death—just the idea of dying. They may seem suddenly interested in methods of dying and the pain associated with each.

Teens who are thinking about killing themselves will sometimes start to give away their personal belongings. For example, a teen who loves music might give his friend his prized CD collection. Another young person might give her sister her favorite outfit or a special piece of her jewelry. In the story at the beginning of this book, Joe Barlow gave away his motorcycle. It's as if these teens are making up their own "last wills."

Another way young people give out clues about suicide is by taking lots of unnecessary risks. Someone who never drinks or uses drugs might suddenly start abusing them. Or he/she might drink too much, then try to drive a car or ride a motorcycle. Teens often seem to take risks while driving. But when someone truly begins to drive recklessly, he or she may be sending a signal about not wanting to live anymore.

Any behavior or conversations that are not normal could be a clue to your friend's true feelings. Pay attention to what you see and hear. It could save the life of someone you love.

Possible Triggers: Problems That Add Up

All teenagers go through rough times. Most get through these times without ever thinking about suicide.

But some young people may start to think about suicide when they reach a crisis point. If problems have piled up without relief, a teen may be headed for trouble. There is a limit to what a person can handle alone. When you or a friend feel overwhelmed, remember that help is always available. All you need to do is ask for it.

Depression: The Emotional Signal

It is normal to feel depressed, or very sad, from time to time. But we know that it won't last forever.

Suicidal teens, on the other hand, are often seriously depressed for a long time. They *don't* understand that their depression won't last forever.

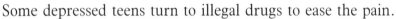

Some depressed teens turn to illegal drugs to ease the pain.

In fact, most think it will never go away, and that death is the only way out.

Depressed teens often withdraw from their family and friends. They may seem very *moody*— happy and up one minute, sad and low the next. Or they may always seem bored and without energy. They might not seem to be interested in the things they used to enjoy.

Depression, like suicide, has many of its own outward signs. You may have noticed this kind of behavior in someone you know.

- No longer taking good care of himself or herself (wearing clothes that are not clean, not bathing or keeping hair clean and combed; no longer caring what his or her room looks like).
- Not eating regularly, losing weight; or eating all the time, gaining weight rapidly.
- Drinking alcohol; using drugs.
- Fighting with parents, siblings, even friends and teachers; not being able to control anger, or other strong feelings.
- Neglecting schoolwork, failing to attend classes.
- Spending less time with friends and family, and more time alone.
- Becoming undependable on a job; calling in sick day after day.

Chapter 5

Getting Help

The office doesn't look like much. It is just one big room in the center of the city. It has a few desks. On each desk is a telephone. Young people in jeans are talking on the phones. They are counselors. You might think they were selling something. And in a way they are. They are selling frightened people the idea of staying alive.

This is the office of Suicide HOTLINE.

HOTLINE is a telephone crisis center. It is a place that people can call when they are in trouble. They can phone day or night. Someone will always answer to listen to their problems. You don't have to be suicidal to use HOTLINE. But if you are, the trained people there know what you need to hear. They know what you need to know to be willing to stay alive.

Suicide HOTLINE is free to the people who use it. The bills are paid by hospitals and church groups. Contributions sometimes come from people who have lost a loved one, or maybe who had one saved.

Crisis centers help troubled people by using *crisis intervention*. It is called "CI" for short. CI deals with those strong feelings that get in the way of thinking about a problem. CI has four steps that help people want to stay alive. Here are the steps:

Letting the feelings out.

Strong feelings are like steam in a kettle without a vent hole. The pressure of the steam builds up until the kettle is ready to blow sky high.

Crisis counselors know you have those feelings. They know the feelings must be let out before you can think clearly about your problem. But first you need to know that it's all right to have those feelings and to let them out.

They let you know it's all right. They often tell you just what you are feeling before you even say it.

You remember Joe Barlow. If Joe had called the crisis center he might have told the counselor that his girl had left him and that he had made a fumble in the football game.

The counselor might have answered, "Those things make you feel very lonely and very angry at the same time, don't they, Joe?"

Notice that the counselor did not talk about the girl or the game right away. She didn't try to cheer Joe up. Instead she let Joe know that she knew how he felt.

That shows the troubled person that the counselor really understands. It shows that someone knows what it's like to feel so angry and embarrassed that you want to die.

Being understood right away is often like a long breath of air to a drowning person. "I felt as if a great weight was taken off of me," says one young woman who was helped by CI. "It was as if a fog suddenly lifted from my mind. I could begin to think clearly again."

Talking about the problem.

Once the person's feelings are out in the open, it is time to talk about the problem. The counselor will ask what happened and when. A teenager could be a victim of child abuse or be pregnant. The counselor will not try to solve the problem. He/she will ask what you think will happen next, and how you feel about it. Solving the problem will take a long time. A lot of other people will be needed to help. The counselor will just help you to bring out all the facts. Then you can go on to the next step. That step is thinking about what part of the problem to work on first.

With the Suicide Hotline, help is only a phone call away.

Taking one step at a time.

There is an old Chinese saying that "the longest journey starts with a single step." In the same way, the worst problem is easiest to solve one part at a time.

The counselor will help you look at all the parts of the problem. He/she will begin with the one that is easiest to solve. A counselor might have helped Joe Barlow by suggesting that Joe talk with his teammates about his fumble. Joe might have found out that they really didn't think about it much. His goof would have been forgiven and forgotten. The problem with his girlfriend would have come next.

Finding and making choices.

The final step in crisis intervention is to help the person see that most problems can be solved in several ways. In the case of fights with parents, for

46

instance, a teen could ask an outside person to talk with both sides. The teen could move in with friends for a while. Another choice might be to do what the parents want. Then the teen could ask something from them in return. The important thing is knowing that there *are* other answers. When the teen knows that, he/she no longer feels trapped. He/she no longer sees death as the only way out.

With the help of the counselor and CI, a troubled teen can believe that the roller coaster of life will end its steep dive and end up level and steady once more. Knowing that, he/she is likely to "stay on for the ride."

CI is only one in a chain of services and people that can help troubled teens. Trained people are ready to help in school, in youth clubs and neighborhood groups, in hospitals, and even in police emergency units. One counselor says, "These young people feel awfully lonely. But really they are never alone."

Remember that CI and crisis counseling should only be done by someone trained to do it. Counselors say, "Dealing with suicidal people is like touching a bomb set to go off. You need to know what you are doing."

But there are some things a young person can do to help someone who is giving signs of suicide. The next chapter tells what they are.

Friends often feel guilty for not noticing the early signs that lead to teen suicide.

Chapter 6

"I Feel Like I Want To Kill Myself"

I t's late. You and a best friend are in a long, serious talk. What you are talking about is nothing new.

Jan has been having trouble with her new stepfather for months. He gets drunk. Often he beats her. And sometimes he forces her to do things that she doesn't want to do.

You have heard all that before. But the next thing Jan says blows your mind.

"I need to tell you something," Jan says. "You have to swear never to tell anyone. I've decided there's only one thing for me to do. I've saved up a lot of my mother's pills. I feel like I want to kill myself."

What do you do now? And what do you *not* do?
People who know about suicide prevention say
this:

Tell an adult—fast!

Jan may mean what she says. She may not. It
doesn't matter. She has told you that her problems
are out of her control. But they are also out of your
control. It is time to bring in an adult. You should
choose someone who has been trained to help. You
can ask Jan if she is willing to call a hotline. You
can help her make the call. You can find the
number in the phone book. Or you can ask the
information operator to find it for you.

   If there is no hotline near you, talk to a school
guidance counselor. Talk to a doctor, or even to
the police. Friends and family could be helpful.
But it is best to find a person who has learned to
handle such things.

Do NOT try to handle things yourself.

Trying to talk your friend out of suicide could be a
terrible mistake. It could mean the end of her life.
The chances are that whatever you say will make
things worse. You might try to cheer her up. You
might try to convince her that things are not so
bad. You might suggest something for her to do.

All of those are normal things to try. But all of them are likely to make her feel sure that nobody understands. They are likely to make her feel all alone. They may do more harm than good.

DO remove all weapons or drugs.

Suicidal feelings come and go. If you can prevent a person from acting for just a little while, he/she may never act on them. Take away the pills, or the gun. Take away anything the person could use to kill herself. She may still find some way to do it. But she might not act at all.

Do NOT keep it a secret.

Good friends are supposed to keep each other's secrets. But not if the secret is suicide! Tell an adult. Your friend may think she hates you for telling. But after she has been helped, she may thank you for it.

DO be a good friend.

Be understanding and supportive, even if your friend is angry with you for telling an adult about his or her suicidal feelings. Try to stay in touch. Keep calling, and stopping by. People with problems need to know that others care.

Friends and schoolmates have to try to understand the reasons for teen suicide. Then they can help prevent other needless deaths.

Chapter 7

Healing and Hope

Even with all the ways of helping, suicide happens. More than a dozen times a day a young person somewhere takes his or her own life.

For that person the problems are over. But for those left behind the problems are only beginning.

Anyone who has lost a loved one to suicide knows that this kind of grief is about the very worst. One mother says, "It's bad enough to lose someone to an accident, or illness. But to see your child die by his own hand is almost more than anyone can bear."

How do people feel at a time like this? How do they manage to go on? What do they have to go through before the sadness can end?

Here are some of the feelings most families suffer when a child takes his or her own life.

Shock

At first most families just don't believe it. They refuse to believe it. Maybe they knew about the victim's problems. Maybe they had heard threats of suicide. But they cannot accept that it has really happened.

For days the mind and body seem in a fog. Even simple things like cooking and eating are hard to do. This is a time when friends and family need to help and keep things going.

Sadness

Death always brings sadness, no matter how the person died. For years a loved one has been there with you. You are used to the sound of a voice. You know the face. You know the touch of a hand. Now that person is gone forever.

A person's mind cannot face that kind of loss without reacting to it. For a long time there is the wish for the loved one to come back, even though the mind knows that can never happen.

People react in different ways to such feelings. Some cry. Others can't cry. Some want to talk about the loved one and the way he/she died. Others can't bear to talk about it. All people feel pain, though. Sometimes it seems the pain will never end. It may seem to go away, but it returns suddenly on seeing a picture or hearing a special song. At last, though, most of the pain does go away. Only the memories are left.

Fear and shame

Sometimes suicide brings feelings of fear and shame. Many people used to believe that suicide was a sickness handed down from parent to child. They thought that if one person in a family killed himself, others would do so too. Some even believed that their family was "cursed" and that suicide was bound to happen.

Now we know that is not true. Strong feelings may be handed down in families, but suicide is not. But the fear remains.

Feelings of shame also remain. Even though the victim is the only person who has done something wrong, whole families often feel ashamed. They feel that the suicide says something bad about them. They feel that other people may think of them as being weak, or trying to cover up some kind of secret that maybe the suicide victim could not deal with.

Other people who blame the family for the suicide may stop speaking to the family. Neighbors may tell their children not to play with the remaining children in the family.

There is no reason for any of these feelings. But we have seen in this book that people often have feelings for wrong reasons.

Anger

Those left behind often feel great anger at the person who has committed suicide. "How could you do this to us?" they say. "Why us? Why now?"

That anger often spills out into other parts of life. For instance, a child whose older brother or sister has committed suicide may suddenly begin to misbehave in school.

Guilt

The mind always looks for a reason for something that has happened, even when there is no reason. Families and friends often blame themselves for the death of a suicide even if it wasn't their fault at all. They go over and over the last words, the last looks. They try to think of anything they may have done to push the victim to act. This hunting for blame may go on for years. For some people it never ends.

Lessons for the Living

There is another kind of crisis counseling. This kind is for those who are left by a suicide. It is meant to help the families of teen suicides and also their friends.

The school is one place that gives such help. More and more schools have ways to help students deal with the death of a friend.

A school in Grosse Pointe, Michigan, is using such a plan. On the day after a student dies by suicide, the principal holds a meeting with all the

When someone you know commits suicide shock is often the first reaction.

teachers and counselors. They learn exactly what happened so that they can tell the students in their classes. That way rumors are stopped.

In the classes that day the usual subjects are put aside. Instead, students and teachers talk about what happened and how they feel about it. Teachers and young people help each other in this way. They help each other to understand the death and to get over it.

Sometimes young people try to make a hero out of the victim. They say he had "guts" to "lay his life on the line for what he believed in." That kind of talk gets shot down quickly. Most of the young people would rather have their friend alive.

As the classes go on there is more talk. And after each one the students feel a little better.

The school also has a crisis center run by trained people. They are on call to talk to any student who feels troubled and upset. The idea is to stop copycat suicides before they can begin to happen.

Over the next four days the school slowly gets back to normal. On one day all classes may hold a few moments of silence to honor the student who will never return. In that way a death has brought many lessons for the living.

Don't wait for a death in your school, or your neighborhood. Remember the lessons you have already learned from this book. If you have any of the problems or feelings that can lead to suicide, get help. Tell someone how you feel. And if a friend shares these kinds of problems or feelings with you, tell someone who can help them.

Most teens never think seriously about killing themselves, even though many melodramatic teenagers may daydream about it. But even though the numbers may be small, the problem is very serious. No matter how small the number of teen suicides, the number of lives affected is much, much greater. Many specialists today have dedicated their careers to saving the lives of young people. A great deal of work remains to be done, but there is hope that these efforts will make a difference.

Glossary —*Explaining New Words*

---

angry   Feeling very mad.

carbon monoxide   Odorless gas that can kill.

child abuse   Deliberate harm of a child by an adult.

cluster suicide   Two or more teen suicides that happen around the same time or in the same way; also called "copy cat suicide."

crisis   Emergency leading to action, a turning point.

crisis center   Place where trained people will help you.

crisis intervention   Way to help solve an immediate problem.

depression   Having low spirits over a long period of time.

emotion   A strong feeling such as anger, sadness, or happiness.

guilt feeling   "It's my fault;" blaming yourself.

heredity   Passing on traits from parent to child.

hotline   Telephone number answered by professionals trained to help with a problem.

mental block   An attitude that keeps someone from thinking clearly.

myth   A belief that many people have that is not true.

shame   Feeling bad because of doing something wrong.

suicide   To kill yourself.

victim   A person who has an accident, or a person who is the object of a crime.

weapon   Gun, knife, or other instrument used to hurt another or yourself.

Where to Go for Help

For help anytime, day or night, use a **Suicide Hotline**. Call 1-800-555-1212, and ask the operator for the toll-free number in your area. You may be able to talk with an over-the-phone counselor right away.

Also available:

Youth Suicide National Center
1825 Eye St., N.W.
Suite 400
Washington, D.C. 20006
(202) 429-2016

National Committee on Youth Suicide Prevention
67 Irving Place
New York, NY 10003

Teenage Suicide Center
Western Psychiatric Institute and Clinic,
    University of Pittsburgh
3811 O'Hara Street
Pittsburgh, PA 15213
(412) 624-0719

Suicide Education Institution of Boston
437 Newtonville Avenue
Newton, MA 02160

National Institute of Mental Health (NIMH)
5600 Fishers Lane, Room 17-99
Rockville, MD 20857
(301) 443-3673

For Further Reading

Goodman, S. "Pulling a Friend Back...." *Current Health 2*, February 1991, pages 18-19. Article discusses what can be done to help a friend who is suicidal.

Hermes, P. "Teen Suicide: What Can Be Done?" *Junior Scholastic*, April 20, 1987, pages 8-10. This article discusses ways to prevent teen suicide.

Hyde, Margaret O. and Elizabeth Held Forsyth,
    M.D. *Suicide: The Hidden Epidemic*, New
    York: Franklin Watts, Inc., 1986, 142 pages.
    This book deals with the tragedy of teen
    suicide, why it happens, and how it can be
    prevented.

Leo, J. "Could Suicide Be Contagious?" *Time*,
    February 24, 1986, page 59. This article deals
    with so-called "copycat suicides" that happen
    after one young person has taken his or her
    life.

"Preventing Teenage Suicide." *Choices*, May 1987,
    page 9. This article discusses ways to avoid the
    tragedy of teenage suicide.

"Teenage Suicide: Early-Warning Clues." *U.S.
    News & World Report*, March 31, 1986, page
    66. This article tells how to prevent suicide
    through awareness of warning signs.

White, W. "Teen Suicide: When Living Hurts."
    Teen, January 1988, pages 70-72. Trys to make
    the reader aware of how desperate teenagers
    can feel.

Index

Accident (suicide or), 16
alcohol abuse, 7, 14, 39, 41
anger, 31, 55
attention (suicide as way to get),
    35

Chemicals (in the body that
    cause emotions), 33–34
cluster suicide (copycat suicide),
    34
crisis, 29–33
crisis counseling, 43, 56–58
crisis intervention (CI), 44, 46, 47

Depression, 14, 21, 36, 40–41
    signs of, 41
drug abuse, 7, 14, 30, 39, 41

Fear, 31, 55
feelings, 11, 14, 28, 29, 33, 44

Guilt, 31, 56

Helplessness, 21, 31
hotline (suicide), 43, 50, 60
hopelessness, 14, 28

Loneliness, 22, 28
low self-esteem, 14, 31

Mental block, 29

Risks (taking unnecessary), 7, 39

Sadness, 54
shame, 18, 55
shock, 54
suicide
    causes, 14, 15
    myths about, 19–21
    prevention, 7, 43, 50–51, 60
    statistics, 12, 18
    warning signs, 38–41

Talking (about problems), 45

About the Author
A native of New York, Jay Schleifer received his B.A. from City College of New York. He taught for five years in the New York City school system, with an emphasis on Special Education. He was editor of *Know Your World* for 5 years, a high/low classroom periodical. He is the author of five high/low books and until recently served as development editor for Field Publications in Middletown, Connecticut.

About the Editor
Evan Stark is a well-known sociologist, educator, and therapist as well as a popular lecturer on women's and children's health issues. Dr. Stark was the Henry Rutgers Fellow at Rutgers University, an associate at the Institution for Social and Policy Studies at Yale University, and a Fulbright Fellow at the University of Essex. He is the author of many publications in the field of family relations and is the father of four children.

Acknowledgments and Credits

P. 2, 8, 22, 30, 36, 42, 46, Blackbirch Graphics; p. 13, 17, 21, 25, 26/27, 48, 52, 57, Wide World; p. 32, Sygma/C. Simonpietri; p. 40. Sygma/A. Tannenbaum.

Design/Production: Blackbirch Graphics, Inc.
Cover Photograph: Stuart Rabinowitz